I0191261

.300 LEWIS MACHINE GUN

FOR THE HOME GUARD

1940 MANUAL
WITH FULL INSTRUCTIONS

The Naval & Military Press Ltd

Published by the

The Naval & Military Press

in association with the Royal Armouries

Unit 10 Ridgewood Industrial Park,
Uckfield, East Sussex, TN22 5QE
Tel: +44 (0) 1825 749494
Fax: +44 (0) 1825 765701

MILITARY HISTORY AT YOUR FINGERTIPS
www.naval-military-press.com

ONLINE GENEALOGY RESEARCH
www.military-genealogy.com

ONLINE MILITARY CARTOGRAPHY
www.militarymaproom.com

ROYAL ARMOURIES

The Library & Archives Department at the Royal Armouries Museum, Leeds, specialises in the history and development of armour and weapons from earliest times to the present day. Material relating to the development of artillery and modern fortifications is held at the Royal Armouries Museum, Fort Nelson.

For further information contact:
Royal Armouries Museum, Library, Armouries Drive,
Leeds, West Yorkshire LS10 1LT
Royal Armouries, Library, Fort Nelson, Down End Road, Fareham PO17 6AN

Or visit the Museum's website at
www.armouries.org.uk

In reprinting in facsimile from the original, any imperfections are inevitably reproduced and the quality may fall short of modern type and cartographic standards.

Manual on the .300-inch Lewis Machine Gun

1940

The Publishers are indebted to
Mr. H. W. BODMAN,
Ex C.S.M.I., School of Musketry
for assistance in compilation

INDEX

.300-inch
Lewis Machine Gun

PARTICULARS OF GUN

Weight of Gun without Magazine or Cartridge Deflector   17¼ lbs.

Weight of Cartridge Deflector   ...   Approximately 2 lbs.

Weight of Empty Magazine ...   ...   Approximately 1½ lbs.

Weight of Full Magazine (47 rounds) ...   Approximately 4½ lbs.

Trigger Pull   ...   .   12 to 14 lbs.

Diameter of Bore   ...   .   .300″

Rifling, number of grooves   4

Twist   ...   A uniform twist to right, one turn in ten inches

Length of Barrel   ...   .   26.056″

Muzzle Velocity   ...   .   2,700 ft. per second

Chamber Pressure ...   Approximately 51,000 lbs. to sq. in.

The primary characteristic of the gun is that of fire power with economy in personnel. Its effective range is 1,000 yards. It is air cooled and therefore susceptible to over-heating. To avoid this, fire should be delivered in short bursts of approximately 5 rounds each. Observation of effect of fire is essential.

A feature of the gun is that the cartridge is under mechanical control all the time which enables the gun to be fired at any angle of elevation or depression and it can operate tilted sideways or upside down.

This booklet is designed to assist instructors in imparting knowledge of the gun and aid the student in understanding the functions of the various parts. A gunner must have absolute confidence in his weapon, and to acquire that sympathetic understanding he should think of machine guns all the time, and know it as he knows himself. The slightest hesitancy in operation must register in his mind the probable cause and immediately suggest the remedy. Unless this complete understanding exists a gunner is not only endangering his own life but he is jeopardizing those of his comrades.

Stripping

In order to dismount the gun the only tools necessary are a cartridge and the spanner which has a screwdriver on end. For detailed stripping, drifts are required.

CAUTION. Care must be taken that springs and parts released are not allowed to scatter. A ground sheet should be used to avoid grit accumulating on parts. The rack and bolt must be forward when stripping is done.

THE PISTON GROUP

Cock the gun and press trigger.

BUTT

Stripping. Press and hold in Butt Catch with the point of bullet, turn butt one-eighth turn to left and withdraw.

After removing butt, hold back the trigger and pull back trigger guard and pistol grip sufficiently to permit the rear end of pinion casing to swing down until it allows the body locking pin to move freely, then slide trigger guard forward gently, using the pistol grip as a handle for body in further dismounting.

COCKING HANDLE

To Remove. Draw back until the rear end of rack reaches rear of body and pull the cocking handle out to side.

PISTON AND RACK AND BOLT

To Remove. After the rear end of pinion casing is released and the cocking handle has been removed, draw the rack (which carries the bolt and striker post) and piston back and entirely out of the body. Then lift bolt off the striker post.

To Strip Piston and Rack. To remove the striker, drive out the striker fixing pin. It is not recommended to separate the piston from rack, but to do so, drive out piston connecting pin and unscrew piston from rack.

To Strip Bolt. Unscrew and remove the feed arm actuating stud. To remove either extractor, lift hook of extractor with point

3

of bullet until the stud on shank of extractor is clear of its recess in bolt. Then pull extractor forward out of its slot.

PINION CASING

The gun is equipped with a pinion casing designed to permit the removal and insertion of pinion and return spring without removal of pinion casing.

To Remove. Unhook pinion casing from the pinion case hinge pin.

To Strip. Press up pinion pawl with point of bullet and allow return spring to unwind. Unscrew tension screw and shake out pinion. Press through the pinion against the return spring hub with point of bullet so as to force out return spring casing. The return spring hub may be removed from the return spring casing with the point of a bullet. The return spring must not be taken from return spring casing except when it is necessary to replace with a new return spring.

THE BODY GROUP
BODY COVER

Stripping. Press both thumbs against the rear end on body and pull body cover to the rear with fingers until the lugs clear their retaining surfaces on the body. Then lift the cover off.

Press the stud on the stop and rebound pawls' spring out of its seating on the transverse rib with the point of a bullet introduced through the channel and hole from the opposite side of the rib. After the spring has been removed lift stop and rebound pawls from their studs. Press cartridge guide down and slide it out from seating.

FEED-ARM

To Remove. Swing feed-arm forward to the right around the magazine post until the front edge of feed-arm clears its cut in body. Slide feed arm up magazine post against key, then swing feed-arm back until key-way is in line with key, then lift the feed-arm off magazine post.

To Strip. Lift feed-arm pawl spring and feed-arm pawl off their posts.

BODY

To Remove. Push body locking pin to the rear with point of a bullet until it clears its hole in the locking piece and remove it. Twist body off barrel (it has a right-handed thread) using pistol grip as handle.

4

TRIGGER GUARD

To Remove. Holding back the trigger, pull guard to the rear and slide off.

To Strip. Punch out trigger and sear pins. Pull back trigger and lift out trigger and sear and spring. The sear spring is held in two recesses, one on the underside of sear, the other at the rear of pistol grip.

EJECTOR

Pry up the rear end of ejector cover with point of bullet and withdraw. Insert point of bullet in the hole in body for the ejector pivot, raising rear end of ejector from recess and lift out.

THE BARREL GROUP

GAS REGULATOR

Lift the end of gas regulator key with point of bullet until it clears gas cylinder casing, then unscrew and remove the gas regulator.

BARREL LOCKING NUT

Unscrew the barrel locking nut from locking piece with the spanner and slide the barrel locking nut forward on the barrel.

LOCKING PIECE

The locking piece is removed by sliding off barrel to the rear.

GAS CYLINDER AND CASING

To Remove. Slide the gas cylinder casing off gas cylinder to the rear. Unscrew and remove the gas cylinder using the piston and rack as a wrench, the cross section of rack is designed to permit this.

RECOIL CHECK

Unscrew with spanner remembering that the thread is left-handed.

GAS CHAMBER GLAND

Turn out of chamber with spanner. The thread is left-handed.

GAS CHAMBER

When the gas chamber gland has been removed the gas chamber is free and may be slipped forward off the barrel as may also the barrel locking nut.

5

Assembling

As would be supposed the assembling of gun reverses the sequence of operations required to dismount. However, with the gun completely dismounted it is advisable to assemble in the following sequence.

THE BARREL GROUP

1. **Barrel Group.**
   (*a*) Place barrel locking nut on barrel.
   (*b*) Gas chamber on barrel.
   (*c*) Gas chamber gland.
   (*d*) Recoil check on barrel.
   (*e*) Gas cylinder and gas cylinder casing.
   (*f*) Gas regulator.
   (*g*) Gas regulator key.
   (*h*) Locking piece on barrel and barrel locking nut screwed in.

THE BODY GROUP

2. **Body and Barrel.** Screw the body on to the barrel and insert body locking pin.

3. **Ejector.**

4. **Ejector Cover.** It must be properly seated or it will jam feed arm.

5. **Trigger Guard and Pistol Grip.** Slip on to body to act as a handle.

6. **Feed Arm.** Press fully over to the left. Ensure that the front edge is engaged under projection in body.

7. **Body Cover.** The stop pawls are numbered. No. 2 has a club foot. Cartridge guide. (Replace after piston and bolt have been moved forward by cocking handle.)

THE PISTON GROUP

8. **Pinion and Pinion Casing.**
   (*a*) Return spring hub into return spring.
   (*b*) Return spring casing assembled into pinion.
   (*c*) Pinion into pinion casing.
   (*d*) Tension screw turned in and pinion wound up to hold it.
   (*e*) Pinion casing hooked on to body.

6

9. **Piston and Rack** (with Bolt on Striker Post). In pushing bolt and rack into body apply pressure on bolt only. If obstruction is felt press back tail of ejector.

10. **Cocking Handle.** Be sure that it is fully inserted. Test by pushing it forward and then try to pull out. Push cocking handle forward.

11. **Lock Pinion by raising Pinion Casing and pushing forward Trigger Guard to engage it.**

12. **Body Cover** (see Reference under Body Group).

13. **Replace Butt.**

CARTRIDGE DEFLECTOR

To attach, turn out deflector clamp screw and pull out cartridge deflector clip. Slide clip and bracket up around body, deflector and bracket on right, so that hole in arm of deflector covers ejector opening. Turn in deflector clamp screw.

To get access to ejector opening, push deflector latch to the rear and swing deflector to side. To return, swing deflector against ejector opening, push latch forward and lock.

To remove from gun turn out deflector clamp screw and pull deflector down.

Care should be taken :

To avoid damage to threads, especially the gas chamber gland, gas cylinder, recoil check and barrel locking nut. Keep threads clean and free from dust or grit.

To see that gas chamber is correctly placed on barrel. The barrel loop of gas chamber is tapered and its smallest diameter must be towards the front of barrel. The vent in gas chamber must be centred over gas vent so that when gas chamber gland is inserted it will centre properly in gas vent in barrel.

That the feed arm actuating stud is screwed into the bolt as far as it will go and that the cam slot in the bolt is slipped over the striker before putting piston and bolt into gun.

That when replacing bolt the feed arm is over to the left enabling the feed arm actuating stud to engage its groove.

That having inserted bolt, piston, and cocking handle, the cocking handle is brought forward to the extreme end of its stroke before the pinion casing is swung up into place and the pinion engaged with the rack.

In replacing body cover see that the feed arm is over to the right.

To check that the tension of the return spring is correct—it should register from 10 to 14 lbs. If the tension is insufficient the rack will strike the butt tang too hard in opening and the action may fail to close, or the gun may missfire. If it is too high the gun will fire too fast, if much too high the gun will not open far enough to feed.

Adjustment of Return Spring Tension

Remove butt and draw pistol grip and trigger guard back far enough to disengage the pinion casing.

To Increase Tension. Hold up pinion casing so as to keep pinion engaged with rack and pull back cocking handle. Drop down pinion casing so that pinion does not engage rack and push cocking handle fully forward. Raise pinion casing, slide trigger guard and pistol grip forward to engage it and replace butt.

To Decrease Tension. Hold pinion casing down so that pinion is disengaged from rack and draw back cocking handle. Then raise pinion casing, engaging pinion with rack, and slide trigger guard forward to engage pinion pawl and the return spring will then carry the rack and piston forward.

The average tension on return spring of gun is from 10 to 14 lbs. To weigh it, attach hook of spring balance to cocking handle; holding back the trigger, draw back the cocking handle by means of the spring balance and as it commences to move to the rear hold in that position and read scale. The tension of spring at extreme rear should not exceed 22 lbs.

When the gun is not being used the return spring should carry only sufficient tension to retain the tension screw in position. In order to obtain 12 lbs. spring tension in the dark or without recourse to weighing, manipulate pinion pawl and pinion so that no tension is on spring but the spring is wound just enough to allow tension

8

screw to stay in flush. Push cocking handle fully forward, hold up pinion to engage with rack and draw cocking handle fully to the rear so that rear end of feed arm actuating stud is even with rear end of body. Drop pinion casing, push cocking handle fully forward, raise pinion casing engaging pinion with rack, push trigger guard forward to lock casing and replace butt.

Care must be taken to hold pinion up tight while drawing back cocking handle by placing right thumb over top of body and fingers under pinion casing, or damage may be done to the teeth of rack or pinion. To avoid the possibility of this occurring when adding considerable weight, pull back cocking handle about 2 inches only two or three times.

Operation

TO FILL MAGAZINE WITH LOADING TOOL

Attach loading tool to a table or some similar base.

Turn magazine upside down.

Slip hole in magazine centre up over magazine post under loading tool until catch engages post.

Spin magazine to test freedom of action, and inspect for damage.

Place a clip of cartridges in top of chute, inserting clip in clip ejector (at right) bullet ends to the left, that is toward the magazine centre.

Press the cartridges down. By putting pressure close to the base they will strip from clips and their points will not be depressed.

If cartridges are not in clips, drop them, bullet ends to left (centre), into the chute.

Repeat, keeping chute full of cartridges and rotate magazine clockwise. The cartridges will feed into magazine.

Should a space occur rotate magazine backward past the vacant space and then resume.

After magazine has been filled, unlatch and remove from post. Turn back magazine centre until it snaps and locks.

9

FILLING MAGAZINE, USING THE LOADING HANDLE

Turn the magazine upside down.

Place loading handle in the socket in centre of magazine. The handle will engage catch and permit the centre of the magazine to rotate freely and independently.

Spinning the magazine on the handle, inspect for distortion.

Inspect all magazines and cartridges before filling.

Rotating the magazine, place the cartridges successively between the separating pegs, the bullet ends passing into the spiral groove in the centre of the magazine. Be careful to utilize every space, as an empty space will cause gun to stop firing. Having filled magazine, remove handle and turn magazine centre back until it snaps. It is then locked.

TO FILL BY HAND

Holding the magazine with the left hand, depress the magazine catch with the first or second finger. Place the ammunition, round by round, in the magazine and rotate the centre block with the thumb of the right hand. Cartridges must be kept clean.

TO LOAD GUN

The position for loading is with the body straight behind gun, with the legs together. The left hand holds the small of the butt whilst the right holds the pistol grip, with the first finger alongside the trigger-guard when the butt is on the ground.

See that the cocking handle is fully forward. No. 2 on left of gun picks up magazine with the right hand, palm downwards, middle finger pointing along longitudinal rib, and places magazine on post, catch to right, and presses magazine down.

No. 1 rotates magazine until resistance is met.

No. 1 draws back cocking handle until it is engaged and held back. This draws back piston and rack and does manually what the gas performs when the gun is actually firing. Drawing the rack teeth over the pinion teeth rotates the pinion and winds the return spring during the entire opening movement. During the first one and one-third inches of backward travel the striker post moves back through the straight part of its slot in the bolt and draws back the striker point from the face of the bolt. The bolt remains locked in its position.

During the next two-thirds of an inch backward travel, the striker post carried still further backward in the bolt, strikes with its right side the cam surface in the right side of its slot in the bolt which causes the bolt to rotate from right to left, turning the locking lugs out of their recesses in the body.

As soon as the bolt is unlocked the striker post reaches the rear end of its slot in the bolt and its travel carries the bolt directly back with it.

The boss of the feed arm actuating stud travelling in the groove in the under side of the feed arm moves the feed arm across the top of the body from right to left.

The feed arm pawl acting against one of the projections of the magazine pan carries the magazine around sufficiently to push the first cartridge down into the cartridge way in the feed arm by the rotation of the magazine pan and separating pegs around the spirally grooved centre.

At this point in the leftward travel of the feed arm, its cartridge way (and the cartridge it has just received) commences to pass under the projecting arm of the body cover which carries the cartridge guide spring, and this spring commences to control the cartridge as soon as it leaves the magazine.

The spring stud on the feed arm clears the stop pawl which is then pressed forward by its spring and prevents further rotation of the magazine.

When the bolt strikes the rear end of the ejector it drives it into its slot, thereby pivoting the head of the ejector across the bolt face.

Near the end of the backward travel of the piston the lower surface of the rack at the rear of the bent rides over the nose of the sear temporarily depressing it against the tension of the sear spring which immediately raises it again.

The rear end of the rack then strikes the butt tang, terminating the opening stroke.

The feed arm is now at the extreme left, the cartridge has been brought over the cartridge way in the top of the body into which the cartridge guide spring presses it, the rebound pawl presses against a projection of the magazine pan preventing backward movement and the return spring is fully wound up. Both pawls are now in.

The return spring now rotates the pinion whose teeth, being meshed with those of the rack, drive the rack forward a little until the nose of the sear engages with the bent in the lower surface of the rack and completes the operation.

The gun is now loaded.

11

HOLDING AND AIMING

The Lewis Gun has very little shock of recoil, but owing to mechanical action it sets up vibration which unless counteracted tends to throw the gun off alignment. This can be offset by correct holding.

The Aiming Position. Raise the butt into the shoulder and hold gun firmly in shoulder with both hands, the right hand on pistol grip, with the first finger around the trigger, and the left hand on the small of the butt. Both hands exerting a backward and downward pressure. The pressure need not be excessive and all tendency to strain must be avoided. The cheek should rest lightly on butt. The bipod should be set vertically.

AIMING. The rules of aiming are the same as with a rifle. To aim with the aperture sight, look through the aperture at the target. Align the tip of foresight on the centre of the target. With the sights thus aligned look at the target. In firing at small or large classification targets the bottom of the aiming mark corresponds with the centre of the target.

Firing

The trigger has only one pressure and this should be taken by squeezing the hand on the pistol grip.

The normal rate of fire is five bursts a minute.

The firer should observe the strike of the shots with as little movement of the head as possible and aim should be corrected if necessary. Accuracy is essential. The sequence is " AIM—FIRE —OBSERVE—RE-AIM."

Allowance for wind will be made by aiming off.

In the case of moving targets aim will be laid on the line of movement in front of the target and fire should be opened just as target approaches to the estimated lead.

Long bursts should be fired and a new point of aim selected for each burst.

MECHANISM

When the trigger is pressed the sear is depressed clear of the bent in the rack. The return spring is then free to unwind and the teeth on the pinion being engaged with those on the rack, the piston and bolt are carried forward. The striker post bearing against the left side of the cammed slot in the bolt carries the bolt forward until the locking lugs are in line with the locking recesses in the body, when the bolt is rotated and locked.

The striker post then continues its forward movement until the striker passes through the face of the bolt and strikes the cartridge cap, exploding the charge.

As the bolt moves forward the top of its face strikes the base of the cartridge in the feedway carrying it forward and downward into the chamber. The extractors then spring over and grip the rim of the cartridge.

During the forward movement the boss on the feed arm actuating stud, passing through the groove in the tail of the feed arm, moves the latter to the right.

The feed arm pawl rides over a projection on the magazine and engages behind it in position to rotate the magazine in the next backward movement.

The stud of the feed arm pawl spring bears against the front of the stop pawl, forcing it back in order that the magazine may be free to rotate.

The left side of the bolt face strikes against the head of the ejector which pivots on its stud and the tail is forced out into the bolt-way ready for the next backward movement.

ACTION OF GASES

Some of the gases following the bullet pass through the gas vent into the gas chamber thence through the rear hole in the gas regulator and strike the head of the piston, driving it to the rear.

ACTION OF TRIGGER

So long as the trigger is held back the gun will continue to fire by the alternate action of the gases and return spring until the magazine is empty.

On releasing the trigger, the nose of the sear is forced up by the sear spring and engages with the bent of the piston in the next forward movement thus holding the piston and bolt to the rear.

ACTION OF MAGAZINE

When the magazine is empty the piston will stop forward and the magazine can then be rotated freely.

UNLOADING (BY FIRING)

First remove the magazine from the post and pass it under the gun. Raising the butt to the shoulder, press trigger, cock gun and again press trigger.

On completion, the firer (during training or on range) will stand up and report " Gun Clear."

UNLOADING (WITHOUT FIRING)

Remove magazine. Hold cocking handle with left hand, press trigger, and ease cocking handle forward slowly, pushing cartridge from feedway into bolt-way. Then pull back cocking handle fully to the rear until the sear engages the bent, and raise safety. With point of dummy bullet press through slot in body against cartridge and remove through the ejector opening.

The greatest care must be exercised to avoid the striker coming into contact with the primer of cartridge.

After unloading, cock, and press trigger to ensure that gun is unloaded.

ACTION OF SAFETY CATCH

When the gun is loaded the raising of the safety catch will secure the gun against accidental firing.

After lifting the safety catch the trigger should be pressed, allowing the cocking handle to move slightly forward thus taking the weight off the sear and sear pin. The cocking handle will then pass into the undercut recess in the rear slot of the safety catch.

To prepare for action the cocking handle is drawn to the rear so that the nose of the sear engages the bent on the rack and the safety catch may then be pressed down and the gun is ready to fire.

Care and Cleaning

DAILY

Cock the gun and clean the barrel with cleaning rod, as for the rifle. A film of oil should be left on the barrel after cleaning.

See that all other parts of the gun are clean and that the working parts are lightly oiled to ensure smooth movement.

BEFORE FIRING

Strip completely.

Clean and remove oil from the following parts :—

Barrel, gas chamber, gas cylinder, head of piston and piston rings, and bolt face.

Slightly oil the working parts behind the body locking pin and smear striker post and cammed slot of bolt with graphite grease.

See that gas regulator is properly set (small No. 1 hole to the rear).

Adjust the return spring tension to 10-14 lbs.

Test feed arm, stop, and rebound pawls, to see that they are functioning correctly.

Examine magazines and ammunition when filling.

Examine and check up spare parts.

See that oil bottle is filled.

DURING FIRING

During temporary cessation, unload and oil working parts if necessary. Refill empty and partly filled magazines.

Ease gas regulator to prevent " seizing " of threads.

Check tension of return spring.

Place full magazine on gun and reload.

AFTER FIRING
(IMMEDIATELY AFTERWARDS)

Unload gun, clean barrel and leave it oiled.

Take off return spring tension.

LATER

Strip gun down, clean thoroughly and oil. Clean barrel (as for rifle) using boiling water, if available, and leave oiled.

Clean gas cylinder with wire brush and mop. Clean other parts with oily rag, and, if required, lightly scrape fouling from gas chamber and all gas parts. Paraffin oil will assist in removing fouling.

Dry, clean and slightly oil.

Examine and clean magazines.

Report any necessary repairs.

Clean barrel thoroughly each day until fouling has ceased and leave oily.

Summary of Lewis Gun Action

BACKWARD ACTION

Action of			*Operates*
Gas	...	...	... Piston and Rack.
Piston and Rack	...	...	... Return spring and stopped by Butt Tang.
Striker Post ...	...	...	... Unlocks Bolt and carries it to the rear.
Bolt	...	...	... Extracts empty cartridge, operates Feed Arm and Ejector, stopped by Butt Tang.
Feed Arm ...	...	...	... Rotates Magazine, releases Stop Pawl, carries Cartridge.
Magazine ...	...	...	... Feeds Cartridge into Feed Arm and the next one into position, forces Rebound Pawl to rear.

FORWARD ACTION

Action of			*Operates*
Return Spring	...	...	... Piston and Striker Post.
Piston Rack and Striker Post	...		... Bolt locked and round fired.
Bolt	...	...	... Feed Arm, Cartridge into Chamber, Ejector.
Feed Arm ...	...	...	... Pawl over and behind projection, Stop Pawl to the rear.

17

Stoppages

If proper care and attention is given to the gun, magazines and ammunition, stoppages (other than an empty magazine) will rarely occur.

POSITION OF COCKING HANDLE

Stoppages are divided into two groups according to the position in which the cocking handle is found.

1st Position.   Cocking handle right forward.

2nd Position.   Cocking handle in rear of first position.

These positions can be quickly ascertained by touch. The left hand, with fingers extended, is placed alongside the body and, if the cocking handle is felt on the tips of the fingers, it is the first position, if felt on any other part of the hand, it is the second position.

USE OF CLEARING PLUG

The clearing plug is used to remove a separated case from the chamber.

1. Tap back centre pin of plug and place plug in chamber.

2. Press trigger to allow the bolt to drive centre pin forward

3. Using cocking handle extension, pull back cocking handle and remove clearing plug from face of bolt.

4. Press trigger, load and carry on.

5. The separated case may be removed from plug by tapping back the centre pin.

IMMEDIATE AND SUBSEQUENT ACTION

Immediate Action means the action which must instinctively be taken in order to get the gun firing again as quickly as possible. It is not completed until the gun has been re-aimed and fired.

1. Feel for cocking handle.

2. If in 1*st position*, rotate magazine, pull back cocking handle and carry on firing.

3. If in 2*nd position*, pull back cocking handle, counter-rotate magazine and carry on firing.

18

Subsequent Action means the further action required if immediate action fails to remedy the defect.

1. Again feel for cocking handle.
2. If in 1st *position* :
   (*a*) Remove magazine.
   (*b*) Examine feed mechanism pawls.
   (*c*) If pawls in order, examine striker.
3. If in 2nd *position* :
   (*a*) Pull back cocking handle.
   (*b*) Remove magazine.
   (*c*) Examine chamber, ejection opening, cartridge slot and guide, clear obstruction, remedy fault and carry on firing.

STOPPAGES

For simple reference the stoppages are classified in the following table :—

Position of Cocking Handle	Result of Immediate Action	Remedy	Cause	Remarks
1st	Magazine rotates	Change magazine	Magazine empty	
1st	Defect remedied	Immediate action	Missfire Defective round	
1st	Magazine does not rotate—no feed	Change magazine	Defective magazine	
1st	Gun fires one or two rounds and stops	Examine and change feed-arm pawl or spring	Damaged feed-arm pawl or spring	No feed, magazine does not rotate
1st	Gun does not fire	Change piston	Broken striker	No gas. Live round ejected
2nd	Remedied using cocking handle extension	Immediate action	Hard extraction due to expanded case or grit in chamber	Faulty ammunition or grit in chamber
2nd	Gun fires	Immediate action	Faulty feed	Worn magazine projection or, if recurs, weak cartridge guide spring

2nd	Gun fires a few rounds and stops	Increase gas or take off 3 lbs. tension from return spring	Excessive friction	Likely only after prolonged firing. Clean and readjust tension as soon as possible
2nd	Gun stops again	Change bolt	Broken extractor	Live round fed against empty case in chamber
2nd	Gun stops	Change ejector	Broken ejector	If recurs, increase gas. If gas is increased reduce spring tension by 3 lbs.
2nd	May be remedied if separated case comes out	If not remedied by immediate action use clearing plug	Separated case	Faulty ammunition
Either	Gun stops. Little or no tension felt	Change pinion	Broken or weak return spring	

NOTE—If the gun continues to fire after trigger is released, remove magazine. This may be due to weak return spring or damaged sear.

It will be noted that a large number of the stoppages detailed above can be avoided if the gun, magazine and ammunition receive proper care and attention.

SEQUENCE OF IMMEDIATE ACTION

CAUSE OF STOPPAGE IN BRACKETS

FIRST POSITION

Cocking Handle Forward

TRY MAGAZINE

IF FREE TO ROTATE
Change it. Reload, relay and fire
(Empty magazine)

IF FIXED—will not rotate
Pull cocking handle

IF GUN DOES NOT FIRE
Pull cocking handle.
Watch ejection opening

IF GUN FIRES SINGLE SHOTS
Examine and adjust gas regulator
(Excessive friction)

IF COCKING HANDLE WILL NOT GO BACK
Remove magazine

IF CARTRIDGE IS EJECTED
Examine cap

IF NO CARTRIDGE IS EJECTED
Examine feed mechanism
Repair if necessary

IF COCKING HANDLE THEN COMES EASILY
Put on new magazine
Reload, relay, fire
(Damaged magazine)

IF C. HANDLE STICKY
Relay and fire
(Faulty ammunition)

IF CAP STRUCK
Pull cocking handle, relay, fire
(Defective round)

IF CAP NOT STRUCK
Change piston and rack, reload, relay, fire
(Broken striker)

SECOND POSITION

Cocking handle in rear of first position

Examine ejection opening

IF CLEAR
Pull cocking handle

IF CASE IN BOLT-WAY
Examine ejector
Replace if necessary

IF CHAMBER OBSTRUCTED
Pull cocking handle. Raise safety catch, remove magazine, clean and examine rim of cartridge

IF RIM CUT IN TWO PLACES
Reload, relay and fire
(Defective round)

IF RIM NOT CUT
Change bolt
(Broken extractor)

IF COCKING HANDLE DOES NOT COME BACK
Change magazine, reload, relay and fire
(Damaged magazine)

IF COCKING HANDLE COMES BACK
Relay and fire

IF COCKING HANDLE DOES NOT GO FORWARD
Change pinion casing, complete
(Weak or broken return spring)

IF COCKING HANDLE STARTS FORWARD AND STICKS
Pull cocking handle. Raise safety catch
Remove magazine
Inspect cartridge guide
Replace if necessary

IMMEDIATE ACTION IN REPLACING PARTS
WITH MINIMUM STRIPPING

TO CHANGE CARTRIDGE GUIDE
Remove Magazine.

TO CHANGE PAWLS (Magazine)
(Stop and Rebound)
Remove Magazine, Butt and Body Cover.

TO CHANGE FEED-ARM PAWL OR SPRING
Remove Magazine, Butt and Body Cover.

TO CHANGE EXTRACTORS
Remove Magazine, Butt ; release Piston, removing Cocking
Handle and Bolt.

TO CHANGE PINION COMPLETE
Remove Magazine, Butt ; draw back Pistol Grip. Pull Pinion
down and forward ; release Pinion Pawl ; remove Tension
Screw ; lift out Pinion complete.

TO CHANGE BODY LOCKING PIN
Remove Magazine, Butt ; release Pinion ; remove Cocking
Handle, Bolt and Piston and Rack. Force back Body
Locking Pin and remove toward rear.

TO CHANGE COCKING HANDLE
Remove Magazine, Butt ; drop Pinion.

TO CHANGE EJECTOR
Remove Magazine, Butt ; Body Cover. Remove Ejector
Cover, raise Ejector by inserting point of Cartridge underneath
through hole in Body. Slip Ejector Cover under Ejector
from left side. Press Ejector down against Ejector Cover
with finger and lift Ejector out toward left.

·30 LEWIS MACHINE GUN
1918 MODEL

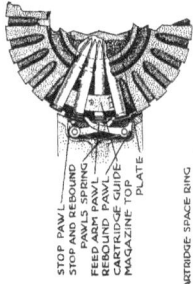

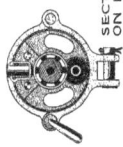

MAGAZINE PAN

SCALE

SECTION ON LINE A—A

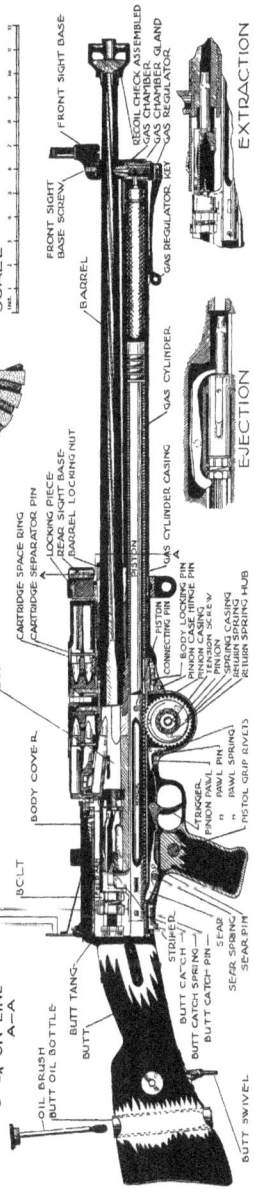

BACK SIGHT APERTURE
BACK SIGHT LEAF
FEED ARM ACTUATING STUD
BOLT
BODY COVER
BODY

STOP PAWL
STOP AND REBOUND
FEED PAWLS SPRING
REBOUND PAWL
CARTRIDGE GUIDE
MAGAZINE TOP PLATE

CARTRIDGE SPACE RING
CARTRIDGE SEPARATOR PIN

LOCKING PIECE
REAR SIGHT BASE
BARREL LOCKING NUT

PISTON
BODY LOCKING PIN
CONNECTING PIN
PINION CASE HINGE PIN
PINION CASING
TENSION SCREW
PINION
SPRING CASING
RETURN SPRING
RETURN SPRING HUB

GAS CYLINDER CASING
GAS CYLINDER

FRONT SIGHT BASE

FRONT SIGHT BASE SCREW
RECOIL CHECK ASSEMBLED
GAS CHAMBER
GAS CHAMBER GLAND
GAS REGULATOR KEY
GAS REGULATOR

BARREL

EXTRACTION

EJECTION

TRIGGER
PINION PAWL
PAWL PIN
PAWL SPRING
PISTOL GRIP RIVET

STRIKER
BUTT CATCH
BUTT CATCH SPRING
BUTT CATCH PIN
SEAR
SEAR SPRING
SEAR PIN

OIL BRUSH
BUTT OIL BOTTLE

BUTT TANG

BUTT

BUTT SWIVEL

www.ingramcontent.com/pod-product-compliance
Lightning Source LLC
Chambersburg PA
CBHW020953030426
42339CB00004B/76

* 9 7 8 1 8 4 7 3 4 8 1 6 6 *